CONSULTING THE FAITHFUL

Consulting the Faithful

*What Christian Intellectuals Can Learn
from Popular Religion*

Richard J. Mouw

William B. Eerdmans Publishing Company
Grand Rapids, Michigan

Copyright © 1994 by Wm. B. Eerdmans Publishing Co.
255 Jefferson Ave. S.E., Grand Rapids, Michigan 49503

Printed in the United States of America

00 99 98 97 96 95 94   5 4 3 2 1

Library of Congress Cataloging-in-Publication Data

Mouw, Richard J.
Consulting the faithful: what Christian intellectuals
can learn from popular religion / Richard J. Mouw.
p.   cm.
Includes bibliographical references.
ISBN 0-8028-0738-0 (pbk.)
1. Popular culture — Religious aspects — Christianity.
2. Christianity and culture. 3. Laity. I. Title.
BR115.C8M68   1994
270.82 — dc20   94-21608
                                 CIP

Contents

The Gospel and Popular Religion

At the end of the sixth century, as medievalist Norman Cantor tells the story, the Western church made a momentous decision: it decided to tolerate magic, fertility cults, and other manifestations of pagan spirituality, thus incorporating some key elements of folk religion into the Christian scheme of things. In making this accommodation, Cantor contends, the church secured nothing less than the very survival of Christianity.[1]

A part of me is uncomfortable with what Cantor reports here. My first response, as an evangelical Christian, is to ask at what price this "survival" was purchased. Wasn't the Protestant Reformation a legitimate protest against accommodations like this? Are we really preserving Christianity when we compromise with the superstitions

---

1. Norman F. Cantor, *Inventing the Middle Ages: The Lives, Works, and Ideas of the Great Medievalists of the Twentieth Century* (New York: William Morrow and Co., 1991), 23.

1

of folk religion? Don't we have every reason to think that tolerating beliefs and practices alien to the biblical message will inevitably dilute the power of the gospel?

But another part of me calls for caution in how I express my unease. Granted that sixth-century Christians were wrong in what Cantor describes them as doing. Still, how *general* was their error? Was it a mistake to be open to popular religion as such? Or to folk magic as such? Or were these Christians wrong in a more specific way — choosing to embrace *particular* beliefs and practices that were in fact incompatible with the gospel?

Let me say right off that I think their error had more to do with specifics than with an attitude toward popular religion and folk magic as such. This may seem at first glance a most unevangelical way to state the case. But evangelicals actually have much in common with Roman Catholics when it comes to dealing with popular religion. At the very least, both get criticized for making too easy accommodations with popular religious culture, and I think we ought to pay closer attention to this fact than we sometimes do in theological discussion. Recognizing evangelical-Catholic commonalities in this area is a good place to start in thinking about the relationship between popular religion and the gospel.

Embracing "Bad Taste"

Here is an example of the confusion I am trying to correct. The Anglican archbishop of Edinburgh, Richard Holloway, recently argued that evangelical liturgical and spiritual tastes have tended toward "fast food rather than haute cuisine." To be sure, he concedes, there are at least some "solid missionary reasons" in favor of the evangelical approach: "More people go to discos than to high opera, and one of the courageous things about evangelicals is their ability to embrace bad taste for the sake of the gospel." But evangelical bad taste is, in spite of its missiological value, based on a weak theology. As a corrective, Holloway points us to the Catholic tradition, whose "incarnational approach" has "bred in Christianity, at its best, an affirming and generous attitude towards human beings, their struggles, their joys, their tragedies and their sorrows," which has led in turn to "the emergence of a Christian aesthetic in worship, art and architecture."[1]

1. Richard Holloway, "Evangelicalism: An Outsider's Perspective,"

At first glance these remarks seem to make good sense. Evangelicals are so concerned to rescue people from their sins that they are willing to tolerate — even enjoy — bad taste in order to succeed in evangelism. The Catholic tradition, on the other hand, has a deep appreciation for the value of the creation, as evidenced in its theological emphasis on the integrity of nature and the centrality of the incarnation. Therefore, Catholicism has developed a "high" aesthetic, which has celebrated the dignity of created reality.

But things are not quite this simple. Are popular tastes not a part of "nature"? Who is really being more "affirming and generous" of our human struggles, joys, tragedies, and sorrows — the lovers or the despisers of fast food and discos? And what "Catholic tradition" is the archbishop thinking of when he lauds Catholic aesthetic sensitivities? Is it, for example, the same tradition that accommodated folk magic in the sixth century?

Most interesting, however, is the archbishop's appeal to incarnationalism in stating his argument. A very different case is suggested by Patrick Ryan, in one of his delightful lectionary meditations in the Jesuit weekly *America*. Father Ryan describes how he has come to have second thoughts about his own early disdain for popular Catholic devotion to the Sacred Heart of Jesus:

> Much as I once reacted against the kitsch in these images of Jesus, I have come to recognize in them a modern

---

in *Evangelicals and Anglicans: Their Role and Influence in the Church Today*, ed. R. T. France and A. E. McGrath (London: SPCK, 1993), 181-82.

folk tradition that crosses cultural barriers. The inoffensive, even weak Jesus with His heart exposed says something to those who might be mystified by a Rouault image of Christ mocked or Rembrandt's justly famous "Head of Christ." Jesus subjected to the humiliation of bad artistic presentation pours Himself out even for those with little or no aesthetic sensibility. . . . How often does the Son reveal the Father in tasteless posters and plastic statues that glow in the dark? More often than I once supposed. The humility of the Messiah who followed the royal style of entry suggested by Zechariah, "meek, and riding on an ass," continues to touch us in the popular imagery of the Sacred Heart.[2]

This is a very different Catholic use of incarnational themes than Holloway's "haute-cuisine" aesthetic. Ryan sees the incarnate Son as affirming and generous toward glow-in-the-dark figurines. Here we encounter a theology of the "natural" that is able to recognize dignity in kitsch.

Patrick Ryan's comment is an "evangelical" endorsement of bad taste — and in the name of the very incarnationalism the archbishop thought could rescue us from a low aesthetic. This should not surprise us. Appeals to the incarnation as such will not settle these issues. We need to be clear about *how* the God who has drawn near to us in Jesus Christ relates to various cultural contexts and phenomena.

Ryan's understanding of the incarnation is obviously grounded in biblical motifs. This is not as obvious in

2. Patrick J. Ryan, "Gentleness," *America* (June 19, 1993), 23.

Archbishop Holloway's case: it would be interesting, for example, to know how he, from the perspective of his "good-taste" incarnationalism, would assess Mother Teresa's oft-expressed testimony that she sees in dying bodies on the streets of Calcutta something of the beauty of Jesus, hidden beneath this "dreadful disguise."

A more intentional focus on the incarnation will not by itself, then, cure evangelicalism of its low aesthetic proclivities. Take, for example, the recent attempt by evangelical theologian David Wells, in his book *No Place for Truth, or Whatever Happened to Evangelical Theology?*, to use an incarnational appeal as a basis for criticizing evangelicalism's strong links to popular culture. Wells is convinced that evangelicals have formed an unholy alliance with various non-Christian cultural forces: pragmatism, a democratized understanding of truth, a fondness for the therapeutic, and so on. All of this is grounded, Wells insists, in an unfortunate state of affairs where

> at the psychological center of much evangelical faith are two ideas that are also at the heart of the practice of democracy: (1) the audience is sovereign, and (2) ideas find legitimacy and value only within the marketplace. Ideas have no intrinsic or self-evident value; it is the people's *right* to give ideas their legitimacy. One implication of this belief is that the work of doing theology ought not to be left to an intellectual elite who may think that they are gifted for and called to do such work and may consider the discovery of truth to be an end

in itself. Rather, it should be taken on by those who can persuade the masses of the usefulness of the ideas.[3]

Christian leaders who endorse such a democratizing perspective have no choice but to "lead by holding aloft moist fingers to sense the changes in the wind." In doing so, they differ markedly, says Wells, from the incarnate Son of God, "who never once tailored his teaching to what he judged the popular reception would be — unless he was an exceedingly poor judge of what the crowds and religious leaders had in mind as they heard him."[4]

It would be impious to disagree with Wells's main point, given the way he states his case. Jesus certainly wasn't a crowd-pleaser who tested the winds of public opinion before he said anything. Having agreed with the way Wells describes Jesus' approach, though, we can still wonder whether Wells hasn't passed too quickly over some very important issues. Is it fair to say that Jesus never "tailored" his teaching to what he thought "the popular reception would be"? St. Augustine once observed that Jesus (and the apostles) performed miracles in order to get the attention of common people who were not yet "fit to reason about divine and invisible things."[5] Augustine was probably overstating the case, but his remark at least

3. David F. Wells, *No Place for Truth, or Whatever Happened to Evangelical Theology?* (Grand Rapids, Mich.: Wm. B. Eerdmans Publishing Co., 1993), 207.

4. Wells, *No Place*, 215.

5. Augustine, *Of True Religion*, trans. J. H. S. Burleigh (Chicago: Henry Regnery Company, 1959), 43.

points to the *teaching* dimension of Jesus' public ministry; Jesus approached people in terms of the particularities of their context. His ministry demonstrates the divine pedagogy John Calvin described in his memorable comment that "as nurses commonly do with infants, God is wont in a measure to 'lisp' in speaking to us."[6] In one important sense the incarnation itself is a profound exercise in divine "tailoring."

Blanket statements about whether we as servants of Christ are to take popular sensitivities into account in the way we communicate do not really get us very far. What we need is a more nuanced understanding of how the gospel speaks to the impulses of popular religion.

I must also try to be clear about what I mean here by "popular religion." Later I will explain why I think that in the final analysis it is a somewhat misleading label. For the present, however, I am happy to work with historian Jon Butler's understanding of the term as designating "no less and no more than the religious behavior of laypeople."[7] Obviously this way of using the label does not allow us to draw a hard and fast boundary between the beliefs and practices of laypeople and those of professional religious leaders. They believe and do some of the same things. I mean to focus here, however, on those popular beliefs and practices that *originate* with the laity. Thus

6. John Calvin, *Institutes of the Christian Religion*, vol. 1, ed. John T. McNeill, trans. F. L. Battles (Philadelphia: Westminster Press, 1960), 121 [I, XIII, 13].

7. Jon Butler, *Awash in a Sea of Faith: Christianizing the American People* (Cambridge, Mass.: Harvard University Press, 1990), 4.

religious trinkets that glow in the dark and Twelve-Step spirituality are expressions of popular religion. They originate with the laity, even though they may be endorsed by some religious leaders — in contrast to trinitarian doctrine, which has its origins in professional theological discussion, even though many laypeople say and believe the Nicene Creed.

I am especially interested in these pages to identify what I think are some aspects of popular Christianity that are too quickly denigrated by many Christian intellectuals. I want to provide some guidance here for sorting out the good and the bad ways of "tailoring" the Christian message to popular beliefs and practices. Sometimes, then, I will be focusing on the relation between popular Christianity and the larger popular culture. At other times I will focus on how popular Christianity relates to specific beliefs and practices of other, non-Christian, expressions of grassroots religion. Later in the discussion, for example, I will return to the question of folk magic, as raised by Norman Cantor's example from the sixth century. But first I want directly to address the issue of "bad taste" in popular Christianity.

"Tacky" Theology?

At a meeting of theologians I attended, one scholar gave an example of his difficulties with popular religion. "I met this young middle-manager type," he reported. "He was a recent convert to 'born again' Christianity, and he was eager to tell me about his newfound faith. He said that he had come to think of God as his CEO, and that God was working to see to it that his special employees made a profit." Then the theologian gave his assessment of this young man's testimony: "How tacky!"

Several heads nodded in agreement. I found the assessment disturbing. The young convert was obviously a theological illiterate — not at all a rarity in our contemporary setting. Yet it seemed to me just as obvious that this person had had an important encounter with God. And in his world of discourse, to describe God as his CEO was in fact a significant compliment: in his human experience you don't get any higher on the authority scale than the chief executive officer of a major corporation. And in the corporate setting, success in the profit margin is a highly valued commodity. If this young man was looking for analogies from his world of real-life experience that would capture his sense of what God had come to mean to him, hadn't he hit on some appropriate ones?

Was this tacky theology? Perhaps. But, then, maybe there is something to be said for tackiness. We might even think of many of Jesus' parables as a kind of sanctified tackiness. Jesus borrowed mundane images from ordinary life to talk about very profound spiritual matters. He referred to buried treasures, loans, coins, sheep, seeds, oil lamps, and daily wages in a vineyard. To paraphrase Patrick Ryan, it shouldn't surprise us if the Savior who came to ordinary people riding on an ass reveals the Father to some of us in tacky images.

Let me make it clear that I am not willing to *settle* for tacky theology. As an evangelical Christian, I have long complained of my community's reliance on cliches and slogans as a substitute for rigorous theological reflection. But I am willing to live with a little tackiness for starters as a pedagogical strategy. My hope for the young middle manager is that he will soon outgrow the CEO analogy for God. Management and profit are not good organizing principles in a theology for the long haul. But as entry-level concepts, they are appropriate.

We should not equate the young manager's theological formulation with his actual relationship to God. The important question is: Has he in fact encountered the God of the Scriptures? Nothing in his tacky theology tempts me to answer no. People can enter into good relationships for silly reasons. Most friendships and marriages begin with attractions that are hardly enough to sustain the relationship for long. But they are enough to get the relationship started — other forces must then take over if the test of endurance is to be passed.

The same thing holds for the spiritual realm. There is nothing wrong, for example, with a person's entering into an obedient relationship with God out of a fear of hell. It would be regrettable, though, if that fear never stopped being the motivating factor in her obedience to the Lord. One hopes that this fearful sinner would eventually grow into a mature servant of her divine Friend, that her spiritual service would come to be driven by a deep longing for fellowship with the Savior.

Distinguishing between entry-level attraction and what makes a relationship endure allows us to recognize two important features in popular Christianity. The first is the genuine vitality of many lay-originated beliefs and practices. The young manager's concept of God as CEO can be viewed as an authentic, even healthy, entry-level expression of a vital relationship with God. The second feature is the aesthetically "low" level of many of these same beliefs and practices. To affirm their vitality is not to endorse them as full and adequate long-haul features of mature Christianity. I can allow for the vitality and emotional necessity of "puppy love" as an important first step in a lifelong, committed relationship between a man and a woman. That does not mean that I need to feel guilty if I don't enjoy being around couples obviously in the first flush of courtship.

To acknowledge these two factors is not yet to have

gotten a clear sense of what is healthy in popular religion. This can happen only by developing the theological criteria that can help us decide specific cases. Recognizing the importance of these factors can, however, reinforce a certain attitude toward popular religious phenomena, an attitude that manifests itself in what we might call *a hermeneutic of charity:* just as what scholars have dubbed a "hermeneutic of suspicion" helps us take a careful look at things we might otherwise accept uncritically, so the "hermeneutic of charity" helps us take a positive look at things we might otherwise reject without carefully considering their merit.

A good example of what I mean by the hermeneutic of charity can be found in a comment that Richard John Neuhaus makes about marriage. The growing number of divorces today leads some critics to observe, says Neuhaus, that people no longer have a very high view of marriage and family. But there is another way to view the situation: the rate of remarriage suggests that "people may think too highly of marriage, or at least expect too much from it. People get married again, and maybe again, in search of a partnership that lives up to their ideal of what marriage should be."[1]

Neuhaus is not endorsing this "ideal" of marriage as it stands. He thinks it needs serious correction in the light of a biblical understanding of love and faithfulness. But to see this ideal as embodying a deep desire for partnership

---

1. Richard J. Neuhaus, *Freedom for Ministry,* rev. ed. (Grand Rapids, Mich.: Wm. B. Eerdmans Publishing Co., 1992), 244.

takes us in a different direction, offers a more charitable interpretation of the facts, than the pessimistic, even cynical accounts that are often given of contemporary patterns of marriage and family life. And the charity at work here is not simply a bias in favor of positive intepretations of troubling facts. It is motivated by a profound desire to see where God's creating designs may still be at work in our patterns of human interaction, even in the midst of our brokenness and rebellion.

Applying the Hermeneutic of Charity

Because of where I spend most of my time in the Christian world, I want to pay some special attention here to *evangelical* popular religion. It's not hard these days to find evangelical scholars decrying trends in contemporary evangelicalism. They worry about the popularity of recovery groups, Christian therapy centers, church growth workshops, seminars in management for ministers, "signs and wonders" movements, and "power evangelism" strategies. Isn't a widespread fascination with such things a serious threat to faithful discipleship? Aren't evangelicals becoming obsessed with "success" and "technique" at the expense of careful theological reflection?[1]

---

1. For a good sampling of these critical discussions see the essays collected in *No God But God: Breaking with the Idols of Our Age,* ed. Os Guinness and John Seel (Chicago: Moody Press, 1992), and *Power Religion: The Selling Out of the Evangelical Church?* ed. Michael Scott Horton (Chicago: Moody Press, 1992).

These are important questions, and I have my own worries about such trends. I have expended much energy in my own career trying to get evangelicals to maintain a critical distance from much that goes on in popular culture. I am deeply concerned about many cultural "isms" — about materialism, consumerism, racism, nationalism, narcissism, relativism, and the like.

Still, I hold to a "transformationalist" view of Christ and culture. We cannot accept sinful culture as it is. But neither can we simply reject it as altogether evil. Cultural formation is a part of the good creation. Contemporary culture, including contemporary popular culture, is a distorted version of something that God meant to be good. So we must "un-distort" it. We must look at such things as the current fascination with therapeutic techniques and managerial methods and ask how they might be transformed into instruments of obedience to the will of God.

And we must also be careful that, in opposing popular culture, we are not doing so out of an uncritical commitment to a "high" culture that is itself in need of Christian transformation. It may be that trends in popular culture, whatever their own distortions, are legitimate reactions against the kinds of distortions to which intellectuals are especially prone.

When I read scholarly critiques of popular evangelical trends, then, I tend to do so with caution. It seems to me misguided for evangelical intellectuals simply to label these trends as bad theology; we must also explore the deep spiritual yearnings at work in our grassroots evangelical desire for visible and practical signs of God's presence in ordinary life. Granted that a fascination with evangelistic methods and church growth and the therapeutic control of inner lives and managerial technique can foster bad theology; but isn't there at least something in each of these recent developments that can provide important correctives to past evangelical habits? Don't pastors of large congregations need to do a better job of managing budgets and forming effective ministry teams? Shouldn't we explore ways in which sociological know-how can help us reach more people with the gospel? Granted that much popular psychology these days is obsessed with "victimization"; but aren't we also learning much about very real victims — abused spouses, molested children, married couples made miserable by poor understandings of what intimacy is all about — who have often been hidden from sight, even in our own evangelical communities?

Why are so many theologians inclined simply to denounce these phenomena rather than to work to establish them on more solid theological foundations? Some of these scholars, I suspect, simply do not like popular evangelicalism very much. Others are convinced that the basic currents of popular religion are so misguided that it is useless to try to look for positive signs. For whatever reason, many Christian thinkers feel no obligation to find points of contact between their own scholarly formulations and the expressed desires and interests of ordinary Christians. They see the yearnings and explorations at work in popular religion primarily as phenomena that need to be corrected, rather than as posing an agenda for constructive theological consideration. They approach popular religion with a hermeneutic of suspicion instead of a hermeneutic of charity.

A more charitable approach will treat popular religion as an important *starting point* for theological reflection. At the very least, we must see it as a good first step in *missiological* reflection. Even the archbishop of Edinburgh concedes this: we need to give some positive attention to bad taste, he says, "for the sake of the gospel."

This concession is better than nothing, but if it is all we have, we will miss out on some important theological opportunities. To think of popular culture as a starting point purely for evangelism is to fail to explore popular religion for all that it might reveal.

Consider how a more expansive view of the importance of popular culture can help us understand non-Western cultures. As theologian Kosuke Koyama argues in his *Waterbuffalo Theology,* thinking theologically about the everyday cultural patterns of rural Northern Thailand is not only a good first step for evangelism; it also yields important theological insights that would probably not be gained simply by doing professional theology in a purely academic setting. Exegeting a Thai farmer's questions and answers about God and nature expands our understanding of how divine revelation addresses the human condition.[2] This kind of theological reflection on indigenous cultures is not merely a form of *reaching out* with the gospel; it is also a way of *gathering in* theological insights.

2. Kosuke Koyama, *Waterbuffalo Theology* (Maryknoll, N.Y.: Orbis Books, 1974), 91.

Many theologians these days would endorse some version of this argument. But they are more likely to show appreciation for a popular religious culture when it is located in, say, a Third World context than when it is close to home. In this sense, theologians are guilty of the same inconsistencies that anthropologists George Marcus and Michael Fischer have complained about in the habits of their colleagues: namely, that, ironically, in dealing with their own domestic cultures

> they are careless precisely about that which would be sacred to the anthropologists in considering other cultures — indigenous commentaries. For the most part, anthropologists have taken the job of reflecting back upon ourselves much less seriously than that of probing other cultures.[3]

Applying this point to our own subject, we can say that North American popular religious culture should be thought of as a form of indigenous theological commentary, which can, when properly reflected upon, enrich our understanding of God's dealings with humankind.

3. George E. Marcus and Michael M. J. Fischer, *Anthropology as Cultural Critique: An Experimental Moment in the Human Sciences* (Chicago: University of Chicago Press, 1986), 111.

Reflection: The Spiritual Significance of Las Vegas

As I write this, I have been reading about some garish new establishments opening in Las Vegas. It is easy to poke fun at Nevada's best-known city. Las Vegas is an easy target for the barbs of its cultured despisers. I have heard it many times: Las Vegas specializes in tackiness. Is there any way of saying a good theological word about this city, which seems to be a paradigm of bad taste?

Las Vegas is certainly fair game for theological critique. Indeed, it is one of the more "ecumenical" topics for prophetic denunciation. Christian conservatives hate Las Vegas because of its gambling, booze, and promiscuity; liberals because of its greed, bad taste, and sexism.

But Las Vegas is also an interesting topic for calmer theological reflection. This occurred to me one day after I read a Travel Section article in the Sunday paper; it was by a bored journalist who decided to justify a weekend trip to Vegas by writing a snide first-person piece about some of the things that especially offended his aesthetic sensitivities. The significance of something in his account hit me for the first time, even though it is a very familiar theme in descriptions of Las Vegas. Once you are inside a hotel-casino complex, the reporter wrote, you lose all sense of time; it is difficult to know, for example, whether it is early afternoon or the middle of the night.

While reading this account, a few lines played in my head from a favorite hymn we sang as children in a Christian school.

> In the land of fadeless day
> stands the City Foursquare
> it shall never pass away
> for there is no night there.

My theological point should already be obvious. Some of the things people mention when they talk about Las Vegas are also things the Bible says about the New Jerusalem — which in its own way is also a glittering, opulent, bustling center of never-ending festivity.

This matchup should not surprise us. Las Vegas may be a very wicked city. But it is precisely in its wickedness that it is also a significant spiritual environment. People go to Las Vegas with deep yearnings for security and satisfaction. It is a place that symbolizes promise. Its psychic currency is the stuff of which our dreams are made. Here is a case where popular glitzy culture reveals some important things about the human quest.

I must confess that in thinking about Las Vegas as a phenomenon of popular culture, I am not thinking just about other people's popular culture. I feel its lure within my own soul. When I look down on its glittering lights from a plane window on a late flight home, or when I catch my first glimpse of it rising up out of the desert as we approach it by car on a trip east, I sense not just its superficial temptations but some of its deeper spiritual impulses as well. This is to be expected. Las Vegas is a counterfeit version of the New Jerusalem. And it shares something of the glorious reality that it mocks.

But it does not deliver on its promises. It cannot really chase the night away or put an end to our sorrows. No genuine security or satisfaction is to be found within its dazzling casino walls. It does not quiet the profound restlessness of our hearts.

*   *   *

My wife and I stayed in a Las Vegas hotel once on the first night of a vacation trip to Idaho. We spent an hour or so on a walking tour. Entering one casino, we came upon a family in turmoil. The father had just discovered that his wallet was missing. A look of horror came over him, and suddenly he began to run. His wife screamed after him hysterically; the two children, one a teenager, began to cry. As we walked away, I looked up and saw a sign bearing the name of one of Las Vegas's establishments — "The Mirage."

"The Sense of the Faithful"

The disdain many Christian scholars show toward domestic popular religious culture is itself a theological defect, stemming from a failure to develop an adequate theological understanding of ordinary religious people. Recent Roman Catholic thought has begun to remedy this defect with its focus on the role of "the sense of the faithful" in theological development — a topic given surprisingly little treatment by Protestant theologians.

The notion that the laity's perspective should be taken into account in assessing a theological or ethical teaching is not entirely new to Catholic theology, but in the past the laity was assigned a fairly passive role in theological formulation. Cardinal Newman was signaling a new emphasis on the laity's active role in the process when he wrote in the nineteenth century that church leaders must take seriously "a sort of instinct, or *phronēma,* deep in the bosom of the mystical body of Christ."[1]

1. Newman, "On Consulting the Faithful in Matters of Doctrine,"

Before the nineteenth century, as Edmund Dobbin points out in his excellent overview of the topic, the preferred term seemed to be *consensus fidelium* rather than *sensus fidelium* — the "consent" rather than the "sense" of ordinary "faithful" believers. The distinction is not a minor one:

> *sensus* refers to the active discerning, or capability of discerning, the content of faith, whereas *consensus* is the "consensual" result of that discerning. The nineteenth century theology of the sensus fidelium was [still] more concerned with the resulting consensus as criterion of tradition than with the power of discernment which gave rise to it.[2]

It is this more active version of the faithful's "sense" that has been given special attention in post–Vatican II discussions of the laity's role in theological development. Cardinal Newman's use of *phronēma*, an allusion to Aristotle's virtue of *phronēsis*, is significant for understanding this role. Dobbin's summary of this point is helpful:

> For Aristotle, and Thomas Aquinas after him, *phronēsis* (prudence) was the intellectual virtue which guided the process of moral deliberation culminating in the event of decision. It was more than a final, tactful finessing of

in *Conscience, Consensus, and the Development of Doctrine: Revolutionary Texts by John Henry Cardinal Newman,* with Commentary and Notes by James Gaffney (New York: Doubleday, 1992), 406.

2. Edmund Dobbin, "Sensus Fidelium Reconsidered," *New Theology Review,* vol. 2, no. 2 (August 1989), 50.

general principles to fit complicated concrete situations. It was more than the application of general principles to concrete cases. Rather, it was the discovery of the concrete moral imperative in the call of the particular situation. General principles and concrete moral paradigms were important in this process, but even more fundamental were the cultivated habits of virtue which, under the aegis of *phronēsis,* homed in on the concrete good being willed. . . . [T]his process of moral discernment could never be fully thematized or adequately formulated or justified in theoretical form. Hence Aristotle's criterion for moral judgment was the virtuous, prudent person.[3]

The meaning of Newman's remark taken as a statement about *moral* deliberation, then, is fairly obvious: there resides, deep in the bosom of Christ's mystical body, a profound practical moral wisdom. Laypeople possess an important share of this discerning power, and no account of what is Christianly right and wrong is adequate without taking into consideration the laity's prudent sense of how our moral prescriptions are to be lived out in the concrete realities of practical existence.

But since Newman's formulation appears in an essay entitled "On Consulting the Faithful in Matters of Doctrine," we presumably may extend his meaning into the realm of *theological* deliberation. So it is fair to interpret Newman as saying that there resides, deep in the bosom of Christ's mystical body, a profound practical *theological*

3. Dobbin, "Sensus," 57.

wisdom. Laypeople possess an important share of this discerning power, and no account of what is *theologically* true or false is adequate without taking into consideration the laity's prudent sense of how our doctrines are to be lived out in the concrete realities of practical existence.

Catholic thinkers are getting at the same issues when they talk about the church's "reception" of a theological teaching. An important part of what goes on in the propagating of the faith is that the teaching actually "takes" in the hearts and minds of the people. If the church sets forth something as true, it will be a good sign of its truth that it is actually *received as true* by the membership. For Cardinal Newman, and for many more recent Catholic thinkers, this emphasis is grounded in a profound respect for the laity's practical wisdom. It's not just that it is good to have them on board when we are clarifying the mind of the church; their deep practical grasp of spiritual matters is an important resource for the church's theological task.

A Protestant Endorsement

I agree with Newman's formulation. That may seem a strange endorsement, coming from a Calvinist. After all, we Calvinists have a reputation for being quite pessimistic about human nature. We believe that human beings have a strong tendency to wander from the path of truth and righteousness. Why, then, place any emphasis at all on an "instinct" for wisdom in ordinary people? Doesn't popular religion need to be monitored very carefully by leaders well trained in the nuances of orthodox theology?

This pessimism about the laity is rooted, as I see it, in a failure to think carefully about the implications of two basic Calvinist themes: God's sovereignty and human depravity.

God is the sovereign creator and ruler of all things. He has placed his stamp on all that he has created. "The heavens are telling the glory of God; and the firmament proclaims his handiwork" (Psalm 19:1). In a very special way, God has stamped human beings with his imprint: we are fashioned in God's image and likeness. We are created to glorify God, to live in an obedient relationship with him. Nothing that we do can eradicate this divine imprint. As St. Augustine put it in a much-quoted passage, our hearts are restless until they rest in God.

Popular religion is the experience of people who bear God's image. Even at its worst, popular religion is an expression of the restlessness of human beings who — try as they might — cannot escape being creatures of the living God. To take popular religion seriously, then, is to pay very special attention to the ways in which God's children — even God's rebellious children — try to deal with needs that are deeply implanted in their created natures.

Human beings are indeed depraved. We have all strayed from the way of truth and righteousness. Left to our own designs, nothing can get us back on the right path. Only God's grace can rescue us. We are all in the same condition. But this means that educated people are in no better position than the uneducated. Theologians have no better access to God than do farmers and waitresses. We all desperately need God's mercy. And we all need other Christians, to encourage and admonish and nurture each other in our attempts to respond appropriately to God's sovereign grace. From my Calvinist point of view, then, Newman is right in his insistence that theologians take seriously the deep theological impulses that are at work in the larger Christian community.

Newman's views on this subject would have been embraced enthusiastically by one of my Calvinist heroes in the faith — and a younger contemporary of Newman — the great Dutch theologian-statesman Abraham Kuyper. Kuyper's credentials as a representative of "high" culture were impeccable: university founder, author of major theological works, political leader who served for a time as prime minister of the Netherlands. But he also regularly expressed an almost mystical sense of solidarity with what he referred to affectionately as "the little people" (*de kleine luyden*), treating their theological-spiritual sensitivities as an important touchstone for his own theological reflection.

Kuyper's views on this subject were shaped by at least three concerns, each of them instructive for our discussion here. The first was his deep conviction that ordinary Christians have often functioned as preservers of theological truth during times of heresy. He experienced this in a profoundly personal way during his first career as a Reformed pastor. Kuyper graduated from the University of Leiden as a self-proclaimed theological Modernist. When he entered his first pastorate in the village of Beesd, he encountered some pious Calvinist parishioners, especially Pietje Baltus, an uneducated miller's daughter, who strongly opposed his liberal preaching. Much to his own surprise, Kuyper was attracted by the faith of these simple folk and experienced a profound evangelical conversion. Here is how he described the situation several years later:

I did not set myself against them, and I still thank my God that I made the choice I did. Their unwavering persistence has been a blessing for my heart, the rise of the morning star in my life. In their simple language, they brought me to that absolute conviction in which alone my soul can find rest — the adoration and exaltation of a God who works all things, both to do and to will, according to his good pleasure.[1]

This deep experience of the laity's important theological ministry to church leaders, as preservers of truth during times of doctrinal decline, is an important factor to take into account in understanding the scope of the laity's practical wisdom.

A second factor was more political in nature. Kuyper insisted that Calvinism is profoundly democratic in its understanding of human relationships. The Calvinists' proclamation that God alone is sovereign has an important social-political corollary: no human power or office can claim the kind of sovereign authority that belongs only to God. Totalitarianism, whether in the civic or in the ecclesiastical realm, is unacceptable. Every human being is directly responsible to the Creator. This is why, as Kuyper explained to his Princeton audience when he delivered the Stone Lectures in 1898, Calvinists have been so insistent on the doctrine of predestination:

1. Quoted in L. Praamsma, *Let Christ Be King: Reflections on the Life and Times of Abraham Kuyper* (Jordan Station, Ontario: Paideia Press, 1985), 49.

not for the sake of separating man from man, nor in the interest of personal pride, but in order to guarantee from eternity to eternity, to our inner self, a direct and immediate communion with the Living God.[2]

It is worth noting that this political theme need not be so closely linked to Calvinist motifs. Evangelical historian Nathan Hatch has given a compelling account of various "decentralizing" populist strands of American Christianity, many of them decidedly non-Calvinist, which are "fed by the passions of ordinary people and express traditional values of localism, direct democracy, ruralism, and individualism," and have thus preserved a healthy "ability to communicate with people at the culture's edge and to give them a sense of personal access to knowledge, truth, and power."[3]

A third factor was Kuyper's strong insistence that God's sovereign rule extends over all spheres of human interaction. This means that our theological grasp of how God relates to the creation cannot be narrowly construed. Theology must deal with all of life; it has as much to do with families and businesses as it does with the Trinity and the sacraments. This, too, reinforces Kuyper's democratic convictions:

> If Calvinism places our entire human life immediately before God, then it follows that all men or women, rich

2. Abraham Kuyper, *Lectures on Calvinism* (Grand Rapids, Mich.: Wm. B. Eerdmans Publishing Co., 1931), 21.

3. Nathan O. Hatch, *The Democratization of American Christianity* (New Haven, Conn.: Yale University Press, 1989), 212.

31

or poor, weak or strong, dull or talented, as creatures of God, and as lost sinners, have no claim whatsoever to lord over one another, and that we stand as equals before God, and consequently equal as man to man.[4]

What is at work here is no naive egalitarianism. Kuyper's primary concern is not to "level" humankind but to insist that since "our entire human life" falls directly under the divine gaze, all of our activities in the creation — political, familial, economic, aesthetic, and the like — must be done in obedience to the Creator's will. In this sense he was not far from the spirit of that "long tradition of democratic Christianity in America" described by Hatch, a tradition whose adherents, exemplified in recent years in the pentecostal and fundamentalist movements, have refused to "surrender to learned experts the right to think for themselves . . . [and] have taken the faith into their own hands and molded it according to the aspirations of everyday life."[5]

4. Kuyper, *Lectures,* 27.
5. Hatch, *Democratization,* 219.

"Postmodern" Laity

Charles Haddon Spurgeon felt deeply indebted to Mary King. She was a cook by trade; but the great pulpiteer considered her a gifted theologian. "I do believe," he testified, "that I learnt more from her than I should have learned from any six doctors of divinity of the sort we have nowadays." Spurgeon continued: "There are some Christian people who taste, and see, and enjoy religion in their souls, and who get at a deeper knowledge of it than books can ever give them, though they should search all their days."[1]

A good example of a "phronetic" layperson. But are there still Mary Kings around? Or have we lost the possibility of producing them?

This is a concern raised by a theologian friend of mine. He has no problem with the respect for the laity shown by the likes of Newman, Kuyper, and Spurgeon.

1. Quoted in Lewis Drummond, *Spurgeon: Prince of Preachers* (Grand Rapids, Mich.: Kregel Publications, 1992), 101.

But he wonders whether things have not changed drastically over the past century. Could it be that what Newman and others saw as a "natural" instinct for theology in the laity was in fact a product of a culture steeped in biblical faith? Because the ordinary folk who prayed for Kuyper's conversion knew the basics of Reformed orthodoxy, they could serve as guardians of a theological tradition that was presently hidden to many professional clergy. But where are such people today?

I have four things to say in response to this legitimate question.

First, I am not quite as worried as my friend is about contemporary laypeople's ability to function as theological guardians. I meet many laity — young and old — who are able to guard orthodoxy effectively even when they are at odds with pastors and theologians.

Second, while, as Kuyper's testimony makes clear, laypeople have often served as guardians of a tradition that might otherwise have been lost to the church, we ought not to limit them to the role of preserver. Often laypeople serve us well as a theological advance guard. I talked to a businessman recently who belongs to a conservative Protestant church that has little appreciation for Christians in other traditions. At work he became friends with a Roman Catholic colleague. They discovered common spiritual interests, so they formed a small breakfast group of business people from a variety of churches. They pray for each other and discuss issues that arise as they attempt to be Christians in their work setting. It was clear to me that they are involved in very exciting discussions,

34

breaking new ground in an "ecumenical" understanding of discipleship. This, too, is an important exercise of theological wisdom.

Third, it isn't clear to me that what those nineteenth-century thinkers were praising laypeople for is a specifically *doctrinal* savvy. Newman talks about an "instinct." Kuyper refers to his parishioners' "adoration and exaltation" of God. And Spurgeon commends some laypeople for their ability to "taste, and see, and enjoy religion in their souls."

These attributes may not produce straightforward doctrinal expertise, but they embody sensitivities against which doctrinal formulations need to be tested. Gifted laypeople have, on this reading, a spiritual wisdom that is tuned into the basic rhythms and patterns of the religious quest. Theology, which attempts to provide a structured understanding of those patterns and rhythms, would do well to invite the insights of that practical sensitivity.

Fourth, what is the *evidence* that shows that contemporary laypeople lack the theological savvy of their forebears? Is it that the laity today are too taken up with such things as recovery groups and managerial methods? Simply to assume that such things are clear signs of theological decline is to beg the question that I am trying to look at more carefully in this discussion.

I am not proposing, let me emphasize, that the laity simply be left to their own theological devices. I am not saying that their religious thought and practice are fine on their own. That may be how some defenders of "democratic Christianity" would argue, but it is not my view. Laypeople need help from professional theologians.

On the other hand, however, theologians need help from laypeople. What I am insisting is that theological reflection must utilize the insights of the entire Christian community; rather than send the laity off to do their own theology, it is important to draw them into a larger process of theological formation. Professional theologians who regularly ignore — even worse, disdain — the spiritual and theological impulses of popular religion are missing out on an important theological resource. Insofar as popular Christianity is the arena in which ordinary Christians are exercising a discerning practical wisdom, a fully adequate theology will attend very closely to their insights. This has long been recognized by Christians involved in youth ministries. They know that they cannot help young people sift through the complexities of the "youth culture" without listening carefully to how young persons experience and interpret the motifs and products of that culture. Theologians must consult the faithful.

I will not offer detailed strategies here for doing a better job of attending to these matters.[2] It certainly seems, however, that some sort of direct dialogue between professional theologians and laypeople would produce some good results. And it is not only laypeople who need to be consulted. Many clergy are much more deeply involved in the realities of popular religion than they are in those of academic theology. Much could be learned, for example,

2. For a helpful account of what these strategies might look like, see Robert Banks, *Redeeming the Routines: Bringing Theology to Life* (Wheaton, Ill.: Victor Books, 1993), especially chapter five, "A People's Theology."

from sustained discussions between professional theologians and the pastors of megachurches. Large congregations are attractive to the previously unchurched precisely because their leadership has a strong grasp of the ways in which Christian themes and practices can be translated into the coinage of popular culture.

But my case here does not rest on the absolute necessity of face-to-face dialogue. What *is* essential is that theologians allow their own reflections to be shaped by the *agenda* of topics that arise out of what Nathan Hatch calls "the aspirations of everyday life."

What I have in mind here is a helpful distinction made by Christian philosopher Arthur Holmes between "theologians' theology" and "world-viewish theology." The former deals with the problems professional theologians pose to each other, "using careful exegetical, hermeneutical, and critical techniques for theological purposes"; the latter treats the questions that emerge in the context of concrete attempts to live out a Christian worldview: questions about the media, selfhood, leisure, technology, friendship, sexuality, politics, and so on.[3] To insist that world-viewish theology is an important enterprise is not to denigrate theologians' theology; nor do I want to suggest that world-viewish explorations are lighter weight than professional ones. Both are necessary enterprises, and when each is done in a vital and creative way, the entire Christian community is enriched.

3. Arthur Holmes, *Contours of a World View* (Grand Rapids, Mich.: Wm. B. Eerdmans Publishing Co., 1983), 35.

"People's Theology"

A strong leveling trend is at work today in artistic and intellectual life. The lines between "high" and "low" are being blurred. Rap music, graffiti, and Nancy Drew Mysteries are treated on a par with the writings of Homer, Chaucer, and Shakespeare as "texts" worthy of literary analysis. Entire university courses are given over to the "sharing" of personal narratives. Where church assemblies once commissioned scholarly studies, they now rely on experiential reports from loosely structured "small groups."

There is something to be said for *some* of this kind of thing. But the general trend is dangerous. There *is* a difference between important and unimportant literature. And off-the-cuff impressions are no substitute for careful scholarly reflection. In many areas of life, we ignore the distinction between experts and amateurs at our peril.

I am no fan of the lowest common denominator. In my view of reality, relativism is a very bad thing. And nowhere do I want to preserve the distinctions between true and false, good and bad, right and wrong, high and low, more than I do in theology. Still, I want to add two clarifications.

First, we should not lose sight of the fact that in distinguishing between high and low theology we are nonetheless treating both as *theology*. I want to stress this because I think we must view the theological task broadly enough to include what laypeople think about. In appealing for the incorporating of lay sensitivities, I have no desire to reinforce the bias, so prominent in much of the evangelical world, against the "high" life of the mind. I don't want to dilute good theology. But I do think that good theology will be fully honest intellectually only if it is open to the broad ranges of Christian experience.

My understanding of the scope of theological reflection is guided by the advice John Calvin gave in the opening pages of his *Institutes:* our knowledge of God and our knowledge of our human selfhood are intimately intertwined. Theological reflection requires, then, that we relate all the information about God that has come our way to all that falls within the scope of human concern. Since ordinary Christians have their own ways of reflecting on how the will of God bears on crucial areas of human interaction, and since these reflections provide important data for professional theological scrutiny, lay theology is a significant component in the larger process of theological reflection.

Second, we should be careful not to be misled by the use of the term "popular" when we make our distinction between what professional theologians do and what ordinary Christians think about. "Popular theology" is *people's* theology, and *all* theology is done by people. Abraham Kuyper was implicitly acknowledging this point when he referred affectionately to ordinary Christians as the *little* people. What made them different from him was not their peoplehood but the "little-ness" of their social status.

A few years back historian William Bouwsma wrote a fascinating biography of John Calvin. He emphasized the relationship between Calvin's psychological makeup and the development of his theology: Calvin's own personal anxieties, for example, fed an intense interest in the need for *order*, a theme powerfully reflected in Calvin's systematic theology.

I find that kind of biographical study helpful. To be sure, we must avoid the danger of a thoroughgoing "psychologizing" of theology. Karl Barth once made a wise comment about Kierkegaard in this regard. It is possible to see strong neuroses at work in much of Kierkegaard's thought, he observed; but, for all of that, what Kierkegaard says is convincing to people who are not nearly as neurotic as he was.

It is a good thing to be sensitive to the very human impulses that give rise to a person's theological explorations. To do so is an important way of paying attention to the basic point of a theological system. This is why I am not embarrassed to refer to laypeople as "little" people with "low" theologies. This can sound condescending, even when the language is used with the affection Abraham Kuyper so obviously intended. But "little" and "low" also get at the kinds of concerns that we have in mind when we talk about the laity as "salt of the earth" or "the grass roots." Ordinary Christians who have not been trained in the technical vocabulary of the academic profession are less likely to distance their religious formulations from the fundamentals — the "groundings" — of human experience. Granted, what they say and do is not the only reference point for deciding theological adequacy. But it is an important place for scholars to return regularly.

And none of us has very far to look, because we are also, in much of our lives, very "little people." We must always stay sensitive to how our theological explorations arise out of our personal hopes and fears. This is why the recent emphasis on narrative in theology is an advance. Theology is not *only* narrative, but it *is* done by people who have stories. To see the relationship between a person's thought and the life-situation that gives rise to that thought is to fill out the picture in important ways. It makes us aware that all theology is "popular."

What I am pointing to here is crucial for my overall treatment of popular religion. Indeed, what I am arguing as a matter of theology in this book also arises out of my own personal narrative. One very important reason why I sympathize with many expressions of popular religion is that they are expressions of my own personhood. I want worship services to deal with the anxieties I carry with me to church. I struggle with addictive behaviors. I sense my own inadequacies as a husband and parent and friend. I have pleaded with God to heal the bodies of people I love.

When I talk about the need for a world-viewish theology that deals with the fundamental issues of life, then, I am not thinking of something that "we" scholars should provide for "them." I am one of the "them" that needs a better theology of everyday life. I want a theology that connects with my *own* "popular religion."

Magic and Biblical Religion

In 1987, D. Michael Quinn shocked the world of Mormon studies with a book that portrayed Joseph Smith and other early Mormon leaders as being immersed in the beliefs and practices of folk magic. Of course, similar allegations had been made in the past by other writers, typically by harsh critics of Mormonism. Quinn, however, was a respected professor at Brigham Young University (he was subsequently dismissed from his position), and he has outdone even the most negative critics of Mormonism in assembling a vast body of evidence demonstrating a clear link between early Mormonism and folk magic.

Unlike the anti-Mormons, however, Quinn does not think that this link is a matter for embarrassment. There has always been a strong substratum of the occult in North American life, he argues. On his telling of the story, the world of treasure digging, seer stones, divining rods, talismans, astrology, numerology, and magic parchments was perfectly familiar to Joseph Smith and his family. Nor did this occult technology disappear from their lives after Mormonism was established.

Nor would that have been desirable from Quinn's point of view. His positive assessment of Mormonism's link with magic is based on at least two convictions. The first is that a synthesis of institutional religion and folk magic is a healthy thing. Quinn obviously believes that the resistance of much traditional Protestantism to witchcraft and associated phenomena has been misguided. If, as he is persuaded, Mormonism was a vehicle for the divine "ratification" of folk religion,[1] then the Mormon movement is to be credited for bringing about an important religious advance in the North American cultural setting.

His second conviction is that in accomplishing this synthesis the early Mormons were being honest about a relationship that has often been the subject of much confusion. Quinn insists that it is extremely difficult to draw sensible boundary lines between religion and magic. The Bible itself contains, on his reading, many "allusions to magic." Referring to the attempts of Christian theologians to establish a clear dichotomy between magic and religion, Quinn cites approvingly an observation by E. R. Goodenough, the renowned historian of Judaism, that it is much easier to classify a practice as magical if it occurs outside of one's own religious setting.[2]

Quinn's discussion raises issues that are important for

1. D. Michael Quinn, *Early Mormonism and the Magic World View* (Salt Lake City: Signature Books, 1987), 35.
2. Quinn, *Early Mormonism*, 6.

evangelicals to keep in mind as we think about the relationship between the gospel and folk magic. For example, he rightly calls us to be clear about the enduring presence of folk magic throughout Christian history. Our Protestant narratives have usually been misleading on this score. We have often endorsed a story that attributes Christian synthesizing tendencies primarily to Roman Catholicism, treating the Middle Ages as a period which saw a series of accommodations to folk religion like the sixth-century illustration I referred to at the beginning of this book; then we have told the Reformation story as one wherein Protestants once for all rejected such accommodations.

We now have good reasons to know better. Jon Butler in his recent groundbreaking study of the first three centuries of American religious history convincingly chronicles the process whereby magic survived the official Protestant campaigns against it in New England. He shows that magical practices were in some cases incorporated into the very churches that had condemned folk magic, as when in the eighteenth century "Scottish Presbyterians used tokens and small cards that resembled amulets to admit persons to communion."[3] The more enduring mode of survival, however, was the "folklorization" of magic in American religious life, whereby "intellectual change, increasing Christian opposition, and government coercion all worked to suppress occult and magical practice in the advancing social elite and to contain it within the rougher

3. Jon Butler, *Awash in a Sea of Faith* (Cambridge, Mass.: Harvard University Press, 1990), 92.

segments of early society."[4] In various ways, then, magical beliefs and practices endured, so that Butler finds in the nineteenth century, for example, "a dramatic American religious syncretism that wedded popular supernaturalism with Christianity and found expression in antebellum Methodism, Mormonism, Afro-American Christianity, and spiritualism."[5] That this syncretistic configuration has continued into our own day has been well documented in recent studies; thus what is often labeled a "new outbreak" of occult interest is in fact a new awareness by elites of a religious substratum that has been with us all along.[6]

Quinn is also right to call our attention to the problems in defining "magic" in a way that will do all that we want it to from a theological perspective. To be sure, Quinn makes far too much of the difficulties here, which should not surprise us, since the blurring of boundaries is important to his overall apologetic strategy. But he is at least correct in pointing to difficulties that need to be addressed more carefully than they often are.

An important distinction that is relevant here is the one typically drawn in Christian orthodoxy: magic relies on

4. Butler, *Awash,* 96.

5. Butler, *Awash,* 226.

6. For a careful case for the persistence of occult beliefs and practices throughout American history, into the contemporary period, see the essays in *The Occult in America: New Historical Perspectives,* ed. Howard Kerr and Charles L. Crow (Chicago: University of Illinois Press, 1983), especially Robert Galbreath, "Explaining Modern Occultism," 11-37. For further discussion concerning the persistence of magic see Andrew Greeley, "Magic in the Age of Faith," *America,* vol. 169, no. 10 (October 9, 1993), 8-14.

"automatic" techniques — incantations, conjurings, spells, sacral objects — that can be relied upon to bring about certain results, while the Bible draws our attention to the transcendent God's dealings with his creation, transactions that have no connection to immanent "occult" forces. Thus the crucial difference is between a magical act, which depends upon following prescribed procedures, and a miracle, which is a manifestation of God's free and sovereign decision to make his power known in a specific situation.

This is a profound distinction, based on an unimpeachable theological insight. And it is a distinction sadly absent from Quinn's discussion. But theologian Colin Brown rightly nuances the distinction when he refers to "the fine but real line between religion and magic."[7] The line between magic and the Christian religion is a crucial one, and it is usually very obvious. But not always. There are times in the biblical record where the distinction seems to blur a bit. Quinn points out a few of these cases, such as Joseph's divining cup in Genesis 44 and the magic handkerchiefs of Acts 19:12. Similarly, Jesus' promise to do "whatever you ask in my name" (see, e.g., John 14:13) and "the prayer of faith" that "will save the sick" (James 5:14-15) bear some resemblance to magical procedures.

Of course, these cases do not prove that the Scriptures enjoin or permit the practice of magic. Those of us who insist on drawing a clear line between magic and the power

---

7. Colin Brown, *Miracles and the Critical Mind* (Grand Rapids, Mich.: Wm. B. Eerdmans Publishing Co., 1984), 276; Brown offers, on pp. 274-77, a helpful and concise summary of the critical issues relating to the religion-magic distinction as they bear on biblical scholarship.

of God have rightly emphasized the need to interpret specific instances of this sort in terms of the larger patterns of biblical teaching. But it is precisely cases like these that have been used, by people who have not kept a clear focus on the larger picture of God's sovereignty, to introduce magical motifs into popular Christian thought and practice. When this happens, we have an obligation to identify what is going on as a departure from biblical orthodoxy. Evangelical theologians have been quite faithful in issuing the appropriate warnings in this regard. Where academic leaders have missed an important theological opportunity, however, is in their failure to think carefully about why these magical motifs seem to be so attractive to many Christian laypeople.

The Importance
of the Middle Range

Christians shouldn't feel too awkward about the fact that the line between magic and biblical religion is sometimes very thin. There are important similarities between the two ways of viewing reality, and in our legitimate desire to stress the differences we must not lose sight of the commonalities.

No one has stated the case for similarities more compellingly than C. S. Lewis in some of his fiction. In *That Hideous Strength,* Merlin the Magician appears as a kind of messianic Christ-figure. The subtle but significant point Lewis was making in that portrayal is captured in a very suggestive passage in the Narnia tales, where one of Lewis's characters refers to the "Deeper Magic."[1]

The Cross is a good example of the Deeper Magic. Because Jesus of Nazareth was put to death in ancient

---

1. C. S. Lewis, *The Lion, the Witch and the Wardrobe* (New York: Macmillan Publishing, 1950), 159-60.

Palestine, my sins are forever blotted out. It seems highly appropriate to talk about this mystery in language borrowed from the world of magic: the "curse" of human guilt has been lifted; the "spell" of cosmic evil has been broken.

The Cross is not *mere* magic, of course. But neither is it *less* than magic. God in Jesus Christ has accomplished more than anything that magic could ever bring about. The Savior whom God has provided is greater than Merlin. The sorcerer's tricks are counterfeits of deeper and more profound mysteries.

It is not difficult, then, to see how to apply the hermeneutic of charity to magical motifs as they often appear in popular Christianity. The Magi in the Christmas story can serve as a kind of metaphor in this regard: their astrological calculations pointed beyond themselves to a greater Sign from the heavens; the spiritual yearnings that drew them into the occult could be satisfied only by the One who passed through the heavens to identify with our deepest desires. Popular fascination with the magical can — and regularly does — function as a substitute for faith in the living God. But it can also serve as a pointer to the Deeper Magic.

In complex ways, the gospel both transforms and fulfills what folk magic promises but cannot provide. If we ignore this promise-fulfillment pattern, we run the real risk of failing to address abiding human needs.

The issues at stake here have been treated in a most illuminating way by Paul Hiebert in his fascinating discussion of "The Flaw of the Excluded Middle." Hiebert tells how he as a missionary in India became aware of a gap in his understanding of the world. He had a "high" theology of the nature of the cosmos, a biblically grounded account of "the origin, purpose and destiny of the self, society and universe." On the other side, he also had a scientifically oriented understanding of the nature of empirical reality. This left him with a middle range of questions, posed to him by converts from folk religions, that he could not address: "questions of the uncertainty of the future, the crises of present life and the unknowns of the past." What can I do to avoid accidents? How can I be delivered from illness? Why did my child, so full of enthusiasm for life, die so suddenly? When Christian leaders are not able to address these questions, the people "return to the diviner who gave them definite answers, for these are the problems that loom large in their everyday life."[2]

Hiebert is convinced that we cannot avoid speaking to the issues of this middle realm. We need, he says,

> a holistic theology . . . of God in human history: in the affairs of nations, of peoples and of individuals. This must include a theology of divine guidance, provision and healing; of ancestors, spirits and invisible powers of this world; and of suffering, misfortune and death.[3]

How do we go about developing such a theology? Hiebert is convinced that we cannot connect our "high"

---

2. Paul G. Hiebert, "The Flaw of the Excluded Middle," *Missiology: An International Review,* vol. 10, no. 1 (January 1982), 44-45.

3. Hiebert, "Flaw," 46.

and "low" accounts with an effective "middle" unless all three levels are expressions of a coherent understanding of reality. This means that we must replace the secularist view of nature as working in accordance with autonomous laws with a perspective in which "God is brought back into the middle of our scientific understanding of nature."[4]

But we must be very careful in all of this, Hiebert warns, not to blur the distinction between biblical religion and magic — a genuine danger, since he, too, is convinced that "[t]he line dividing them is a subtle one." How do we properly patrol this boundary?

> The difference is not one of form, but of attitude. What begins as a prayer of request may turn into a formula or chant to force God to do one's will by saying or doing the right thing. In religion, we want the will of God for we trust in his omniscience. In magic we seek our own wills, confident that we know what is best for ourselves.[5]

Hiebert's discussion makes it clear what we need: a biblically grounded account of God's day-to-day dealings with us in the midst of our practical uncertainties about, for example, our health, our financial resources, and our intimate relationships. When we fail to provide such an account, people — ordinary Christians — will turn to those elements of folk religion, such as New Age em-

4. Hiebert, "Flaw," 46.
5. Hiebert, "Flaw," 46.

phases, superstitious practices, a fascination with angels and demons, which are designed to deal with these very kinds of human concerns.

But how do we develop such an account? It should be clear by now what we want to avoid. On the one hand it will not do simply to repeat to ordinary Christians the claims of high theology as answers to their practical questions. Not that there is anything wrong with high theology. On the contrary, it is absolutely necessary for us to be clear on that level of articulation: we need to know that God created the world out of his own sovereign good pleasure; that the Creator is *totaliter aliter*, absolutely distinct from that which he has created; that the second Person of the Trinity left heaven's highest throne to take our human condition upon himself; that God was in Christ reconciling the world unto himself; and so on. But the proclamation of these important truths is not enough to equip Christian people to struggle with the practical challenges of everyday existence.

On the other hand, neither is a synthesis of high theology and the beliefs and practices of non-Christian folk magic acceptable. And the historical studies we have mentioned show us that this synthesis often occurs when Christian elites refuse to go beyond the formulations of high theology. This leaves the laity to their own devices, with no way of connecting high and low, as in the case, for example, of a young married couple who are having great difficulty relating their "macro" belief in the sovereign Creator and Ruler of the universe with their own "micro," and deeply painful, struggle with infertility.

These are the patterns we want to avoid. What, then, are we looking for? A deepening of Christian *phronēsis,* of the practical theological wisdom of the Christian community. This will not happen simply by adding more nuances to our theology — although that is a necessary step. Nor is it merely a matter of thinking more about the application of our high theology to concrete situations of everyday life — although that, too, is a good thing. The deepening of *phronēsis* requires a strategy that integrates various kinds of sensitivities and insights: theological, pastoral, ethical, spiritual, social scientific. The result to be aimed at in this process is not so much a set of guidelines or concrete decisions as it is the formation of Christian *character,* a how-to-*be* rather than a how-to-*do.*

I will not deal here with everything that is important for working toward this result. I will limit my comments to a few of the more controversial topics relating to popular evangelical religion, focusing on two important sets of sensitivities that need to inform our efforts to deepen the practical wisdom of the Christian community.

The first set of sensitivities comprises *missiological* ones. Hiebert's essay provides a good case in point for the importance of this perspective. The missionary setting has often served as a fruitful context for testing the adequacy of our high theological formulations.

Much attention has been given in recent decades to the role of cultural context in our understanding of the Christian story. Theologians, and especially missiologists, have heightened our awareness of the way our cultural lenses affect the way in which we receive and "package" the data of biblical revelation.[6] In this regard the focus on non-Western or non–"North Atlantic" cultures has had a healthy impact on theological reflection.

It is also necessary, however, to apply the lessons that we have learned from contextualization discussions to our own cultural setting. I am convinced that some of our best domestic contextualizers in this regard are the popular "televangelists" and "mega-church" pastors. In saying this I mean to be turning what is often a sharp criticism of these leaders into a low-key compliment. Their critics accuse them of cultural accommodation, of presenting a version of Christianity that identifies too closely with the beliefs and practices of popular culture. In paying my low-key compliment, I mean to point to the ways in which they have often been very sensitive to "excluded-middle" concerns and questions.[7]

A strong emphasis on faith-healing, the proclamation of "health and wealth" themes, the providing of practical techniques for "successful living" — all of these are ways of addressing the "middle" realm of human concern. My compliment is intentionally *low-key*, however, because I am not convinced that the mega-church pastors and televangelists have always paid close enough attention to the

6. For a good overview and sampling of these discussions, see the essays in *The Word Among Us: Contextualizing Theology for Mission Today*, ed. Dean S. Gilliland (Dallas: Word Publishing, 1989).

7. See William A. Dyrness, *How Does America Hear the Gospel?* (Grand Rapids, Mich.: Wm. B. Eerdmans Publishing Co., 1989), 119-30, for an insightful, nuanced assessment of Robert Schuller's ministry in this regard.

important question of how their address to the "middle" range comports with high theological formulations of biblical truth.

A more adequate theological address to these topics in our domestic culture must make use of some of the same tools that the missiologists have used in examining "exotic" contexts. I want to give special emphasis here to the tools of cultural anthropology. Anthropology is a field of study that has thrived on the examination of cultural differences. One of the benefits of such a focus is the way in which, as Marcus and Fischer put it, "cross-cultural juxtaposition" can serve to facilitate "de-familiarization."[8]

It is a good thing, on occasion, for the familiar suddenly to appear to us in a strange light. To be sure, de-familiarization can also be the stuff of deep alienation (as in Camus' novel *The Stranger*). But de-familiarization can also be something we intentionally strive for, not as an end in itself but as a helpful step toward new dimensions of understanding. It is good sometimes to stand back from things that we know intimately, to try to see them as they might appear to a stranger.

The conceptual tools of cultural anthropology can help us to achieve that step. To study a college basketball game by seeing it as a set of tribal rituals or to consider a teen's first week in high school as a series of rites of initiation is to gain new insights by a procedural kind of de-familiarization. Similar gains can be made by using

8. George E. Marcus and Michael M. J. Fischer, *Anthropology as Cultural Critique* (Chicago: University of Chicago Press, 1986).

56

these tools in order to understand better what is going on in popular religion. To see popular beliefs and practices as parallels to the ways in which people in other cultures attempt to cope with middle range concerns is an important step toward a coherent theology for everyday life.

The Importance
of the Therapeutic

The second set of sensitivities comprises *psychological* ones. To say a positive theological word about "the therapeutic" these days is to oppose some of the harshest critics of popular evangelicalism. David Wells, for one, rebukes the evangelical journal *Leadership* for the image of the clergy that it consistently promotes: "In the study, the evangelical pastor is now the C.E.O.; in the pulpit, the pastor is a psychologist whose task it is to engineer good relations and warm feelings."[1]

Let us take a look at the therapeutic portion of this image, which Wells obviously considers a corruption of the pastoral task: ministers today "engineer good relations and warm feelings." What exactly is wrong with this understanding of what ministers do in the pulpit? Or better yet: What exactly is right with it? What happens when we apply the

1. David F. Wells, *No Place for Truth* (Grand Rapids, Mich.: Wm. B. Eerdmans Publishing Co., 1993), 177.

hermeneutic of charity to this account of what ministers do in the pulpit?

It will be helpful to go back to Paul Hiebert's summary of "excluded middle" topics: "Here one finds the questions of the uncertainty of the future, the crises of present life and the unknowns of the past." People come to church with these middle-level questions. And not just the "ordinary" laity — many of us who love high theology come to church with these same questions. On most Sundays these are the issues that dominate my own psyche as I enter the place of worship: I regularly carry real fears about concrete things that may or may not happen in the next week; sometimes I haven't been sleeping well; often I am "tossed about," as the old hymn puts it, "with many a conflict, many a doubt, fighting and fears, within, without"; not infrequently I am nagged by uneasiness and guilt about the remembrance — and the forgetfulness — of things past.

For those of us who go to church with those kinds of burdens, the expectation that we will encounter a pastor who knows how to "engineer good relations and warm feelings" — even allowing for the touch of sarcasm in Wells's way of putting it — is not such a bad thing. And this kind of experience can be a very positive thing indeed if the "good relations" and "warm feelings" are "engineered" by someone who knows how to lead us into a vital communal encounter with the living God.

Given the kind of people we are, psychological sensitivities have an important place in our worship. To say this is not to argue for a thoroughgoing psychologizing of worship. Worship must include the acknowledgment of

God's glory and majesty, a renewal of our commitment to the larger goals of the Kingdom, the hearing of the Word proclaimed in all of its richness, eucharistic fellowship — it is impossible to contain all of this within the confines of the therapeutic.

But it is also important to reverse the formula: a psychological perspective that is grounded in a biblical view of reality is too valuable a resource to be squeezed into the confines of the worship experience. There is an important parallel here to the issues of social-political life. Many of us are rightly nervous when worship is too much given over to an emphasis on a "social gospel." One good reason for this nervousness is that worship ought not in any way to be reduced to a social-political emphasis. But there is another good reason to be nervous about politicized worship: the social-political dimensions of life are too significant and complex to be forced into the confines of the worship setting. Worship ought to be shaped by, among other things, social-political sensitivities. But that does not mean that worship ought ever to be viewed primarily in political terms.

The Christian community needs more, not less, psychology than Wells's depiction allows for. Ministers ought not to be mere therapists for at least two reasons. First, the pastoral role is more than a therapeutic one. Second, the therapeutic is too important for us to give the impression that it can be contained within the pastoral role. Psychological issues need to be dealt with in one-on-one counseling sessions, small groups, conferences, workshops, and continuing education courses.

Obvious objections to this come quickly to mind. Isn't psychology often destructive of Christian commitment? Yes, but so is theology often destructive of Christian commitment; we should be thinking here not about bad psychology but about good psychology — a psychological perspective grounded in a biblical understanding of the human condition. Do I mean to suggest that psychology is as important as worship? No, very few things are as important as worship; writing theology books is not as important as worship, for example, but theology books are still worth writing. Doesn't the therapeutic perspective encourage an unhealthy introspective preoccupation with the needs of our own psyches? Yes, which is why it is important to encourage a *healthy* introspection; "Search me, O God, and know my heart" — good psychology can help me understand the complexities of the self that I present for divine scrutiny.

But we must probe a little bit deeper in our thinking about the therapeutic culture. It isn't just Christian theologians who worry about the inroads of psychology. Some social critics have expressed concern about the prominence of therapeutic motifs in the larger culture. A good case in point is Philip Rieff, who provided a sustained and influential critique of these patterns a few decades ago in *The Triumph of the Therapeutic*. Rieff explicitly contrasted the therapeutic outlook with a religious one. The "mystic," he argued, is interested in "ultimate" questions; but there is no place for ultimacy in the therapist's picture of reality.

In the workaday world, there are not ultimate concerns, only present ones. Therapy is the respite of every day, during which the importance of the present is learned, and the existence of what in the ascetic tradition came to be called "ultimate" or "divine" is unlearned.

While the older religious views of reality provided a framework for "trying to order the warring parts of the personality into a hierarchy," the therapeutic perspective sees all parts as equal — which means that a healthy self will simply find practical strategies for living with the warring parts by developing "an informed (i.e., healthy) respect for the sovereign and unresolvable basic contradictions that make him the singularly complicated human being he is."[2]

Essentially the same account is given by philosopher Alasdair MacIntyre, who sees the Therapist and the Manager as two of the central roles, or social "characters," that provide contemporary culture with its "moral definitions." He views both as representing an "emotivist" morality, for which it is impossible to engage in moral discourse about the ends or goals that human beings ought to pursue. The Manager is concerned solely with the techniques necessary to transform "raw materials into final products, unskilled labor into skilled labor, investment into profits." The Therapist's "concern also is with technique, with effectiveness in transforming neurotic symp-

2. Philip Rieff, *The Triumph of the Therapeutic: Uses of Faith After Freud* (New York: Harper and Row, 1966), 54-55.

toms into directed energy, maladjusted individuals into well-adjusted ones."[3]

There is much that is helpful, and even profound, in these critical analyses of the therapeutic and managerial motifs in contemporary culture. They raise crucial issues that cannot be ignored. But we must also be careful not to use these critical analyses in an uncritical way. To paint our pictures of contemporary life with too broad strokes can be misleading.

I wish, for example, that my fellow evangelical Os Guinness would make a little more use of a hermeneutic of charity when he discusses recent fundamentalism's "general reliance on both the therapeutic and managerial revolutions." Guinness rightly worries that Christians who loudly denounce "secularism," a viewpoint that denies the supernatural, run the risk of themselves embracing "secularity," a way of acting "that gives no practical place to supernatural perspectives or values." He sees this embrace occurring in fundamentalists' enthusiastic adoption of new technologies.[4]

But does it follow from the fact that fundamentalists make considerable use these days of therapeutic and managerial motifs that they have in a rather obvious way bought into "the therapeutic and managerial revolutions"? Guinness seems to think so. I want to urge some caution here.

3. Alasdair MacIntyre, *After Virtue: A Study in Moral Theory* (Notre Dame, Ind.: University of Notre Dame Press, 1981), 29.
4. Os Guinness, *The American Hour: A Time of Reckoning and the Once and Future Role of Faith* (New York: The Free Press, 1993), 337.

At least this much seems clear to me: it is not enough simply to point to some common behavioral patterns between fundamentalism and secularity, and then conclude that both are working with the same worldview. It is necessary to ask — the hermeneutic of charity again — *why* the fundamentalists are so interested in management and therapy these days.

I am inclined to think that to the degree that fundamentalists really *are* becoming managerial and therapeutic, they ought to be given credit for working on some important weaknesses in their movement. The managerial culture pays much attention, for example, to such things as organizational "process" and conflict management; these are areas where fundamentalist communities have been notoriously weak. Similarly, if fundamentalists, who have in their own ways fostered a highly intellectualized understanding of Christian faith, are now attending to such therapeutic concerns as "being in touch with your feelings" and "listening skills," this could be a major step in the right direction.

And even if Christians are simply adapting to the more general cultural fascination with the Therapist and the Manager, it is not altogether fair to see this, as Guinness does,[5] simply as a compromise with "Modernity." Alasdair MacIntyre's case is more nuanced. He would agree with Guinness that there is much in contemporary life that tempts us to rely on "proven techniques" for imposing some

---

5. In addition to the discussion in *The American Hour,* see Guinness's characterizations in his *Dining with the Devil: The Megachurch Flirts with Modernity* (Grand Rapids, Mich.: Baker Book House, 1993).

semblance of control on both the internal and the external manifestations of chaos. Thus the popularity of the Therapist and the Manager. But MacIntyre also insists that the culture whose moral definitions are provided by these two social "characters" cannot be sustained, because the way of the Therapist and the Manager relies on the false presumption of a genuine managerial and therapeutic "expertise"; the claim to be an expert actually masks the fact that the Therapist and the Manager make arbitrary, criterionless choices. For MacIntyre, post-Enlightenment thinkers must make a very basic choice, as symbolized in the title of his "Nietzsche or Aristotle?" chapter in *After Virtue.* Either they must become honest about their moral nihilism, or they must go back to a premodern view of reality.[6]

MacIntyre chooses the second option, arguing for a return to Aristotelian (and in his more recent writings, a Thomistic) philosophical perspective. But it is clear that in the broader culture other forms of premodernity are also being explored, among them the occult worldview (an important selling point in Quinn's Mormon apologetic). In some cases, as in the "heavy metal" subculture, one can even find a kind of Nietzschean-occult synthesis.

It is important to note, however, that the realms of professional therapy and management are themselves influenced by premodern perspectives, as in the use of Zen exercises and "visualization" techniques in managerial practice and the popularity of the more occult aspects of Jungian thought in some therapeutic circles. In shopping

6. MacIntyre, *After Virtue,* 103-13.

for a therapist these days, one might well come upon many Nietzscheans — but one will also run into a few students of shamanism and Navajo healing rituals! In short, therapy and management are not simply given to the thought patterns of "modernity"; they also provide evidence of a strong disillusionment with Enlightenment thought.

We cannot accuse popular Christianity of compromising with modernity, then, simply because many Christians are now interested in therapy and management. In fact, in the light of MacIntyre's analysis one could argue for a much more hopeful scenario: it may be that Christian people, in their enthusiasm for managerial and therapeutic motifs, are intuiting that a secularist managerial-therapeutic culture is ineluctably drawn toward a thoroughgoing nihilism, and because of this they are working — admittedly, in a manner that is not always coherent — to connect these motifs to a biblical perspective on reality. It certainly seems plausible to see the current interest in these matters as having spiritual significance. As I have been arguing, many people today show an interest in therapy and management with the same kinds of middle range questions that have made folk magic so attractive.

When I read Os Guinness's observation, then, that much of our "increased religiosity" these days "is actually a new secularity with a religious gloss,"[7] I am strongly inclined to consider a reversal of his point: that much of our increased secularity today is actually a new religiosity with a secularist gloss!

7. Guinness, *American Hour,* 337.

"God's Gentle Guidance"

Henri Nouwen is one of the people who has warned us against "psychologizing" the Christian message. His warning is worth considering carefully:

> Most Christian leaders today raise psychological or sociological questions even though they frame them in scriptural terms. Real theological thinking, which is thinking with the mind of Christ, is hard to find in the practice of the ministry. Without solid theological reflection, future leaders will be little more than pseudo-psychologists, pseudo-sociologists, pseudo-social workers. They will think of themselves as enablers, facilitators, role models, father or mother figures, big brothers or big sisters, and so on, and thus join the countless men and women who make a living trying to help their fellow human beings to cope with the stresses and strains of everyday living.[1]

1. Henri J. M. Nouwen, *In the Name of Jesus: Reflections on Christian Leadership* (New York: Crossroad, 1992), 66.

This is a good and helpful warning. But it is also important to attend to Nouwen's description of the *right* way to engage in Christian ministry:

Christian leaders have the arduous task of responding to the personal struggles, family conflicts, national calamities, and international tensions with an articulate faith in God's real presence. They have to say "no" to every form of fatalism, defeatism, accidentalism or incidentalism which make people believe that statistics are telling us the truth. They have to say "no" to every form of despair in which human life is seen as a pure matter of good or bad luck. They have to say "no" to sentimental attempts to make people develop a spirit of resignation or stoic indifference in the face of the unavoidability of pain, suffering, and death. . . . [They] have to be theologians, persons who know the heart of God and are trained — through prayer, study, and careful analysis — to manifest the divine event of God's saving work in the midst of the many seemingly random events of their time.

Theological reflection is reflecting on the painful and joyful realities of every day with the mind of Jesus and thereby raising human consciousness to the knowledge of God's gentle guidance.[2]

Nouwen wants real theology, not social science couched in religious terms. He is right to insist on this. But it is also important to be clear about what real theology

2. Nouwen, *Name,* 67-68.

actually looks like from his perspective. It is a theological reflection on questions of the middle range, a theology aimed at practical wisdom. We are not to help people merely to *cope* with life's quandaries and agonies. We are to *address* those complexities and pains, showing how God's saving work relates to the "seemingly random events" of our lives, so that Christian people can discern "the mind of Jesus" and thereby experience "God's gentle guidance."

I do not see what Nouwen is saying here as being in conflict with the approach I have been setting forth. He chooses to warn against a misplaced emphasis on psychological techniques, a reduction of ministry to social work and therapy. I agree with him. I don't want ministers to restrict their efforts to the therapeutic. Indeed, I don't even want social workers and therapists to operate with the restricted vision that Nouwen describes!

Theologian Ellen Charry makes the case well when she describes "classical theological psychology's clash with the modern therapeutic mind-set." What is at work in this clash is "divergent understandings of need and who determines it." We must turn from our own definitions of the good life to obedience to God, even if the remedy is "hard to swallow." This "psychology" stands in stark contrast to a perspective that sees "need as closer to desire and us as the proper judges of both."[3] As Os Guinness

3. Ellen T. Charry, "Is Christianity Good for Us?" in *Reclaiming the Faith: Essays on Orthodoxy in the Episcopal Church and the Baltimore Declaration,* ed. Ephraim Radner and George R. Sumner (Grand Rapids, Mich.: Wm. B. Eerdmans Publishing Co., 1993), 229.

puts it, Christian psychology must be based on an under-standing of people's "true needs — their needs as God, not the world, defines them."[4]

The problem isn't simply that pastoral ministry is often reduced to the therapeutic. The therapeutic itself is often reduced to something less than a profound address to human beings in their complex wholeness. We need Christians in pastoral ministries *and* in social work and psychology whose healing ministries are shaped by a rich vision of "God's gentle guidance."

Psychology can function "phronetically"; it can aid us in strengthening the patterns of Christian practical wis-dom. Think again of Hiebert's middle area of human con-cerns. Christian people worry about financial security. They grieve over the loss of loved ones. They get angry when they can't produce offspring. They get caught up in deep and inexplicable depressions. They feel trapped in difficult intimate relationships. They struggle with guilt over acts committed long ago. How are we to help them deal with these concerns?

One possible strategy, of course, is simply to teach them the claims of high theology. God is sovereign. God has a plan. All things will turn out well for those who trust the Lord. We grow through suffering. These are important truths, and they ought to be proclaimed boldly. But it is a simple fact of Christian experience for many of us that they are not enough to carry us through the diffi-

4. Guinness, *Dining with the Devil* (Grand Rapids, Mich.: Baker Book House, 1993), 67.

culties of life. And the Bible itself tells us that they are not enough. It encourages us to live out our struggles in the context of a community that accepts the truths of revelation and promotes practical discipleship through the exercise of gifts, such as prophesying, discernment, teaching, and healing.

These gifts help to equip the saints with many good things. But surely the benefits include such practical, middle-level things as coping mechanisms, insight into the concrete patterns of our personal lives, an integrated sense of our individual and collective pilgrimages. Good therapy also deals with these issues. It can equip us to cope with grief and anger. It can sensitize us to connections among seemingly disparate bits and pieces of our lives. It can teach us better to integrate our feelings, thoughts, imaginings, and choices. It can help us to tell our stories in more honest and holistic ways. In short, it can promote the formation of mature Christian character. Good therapy can be one way in which we experience the exercise of the gifts of the Spirit: this, too, is a context in which we can learn prophecy, discernment, teaching, and healing.

It shouldn't be taken as just a silly joke when clever people refer to therapists as the witch doctors and exorcists of our high-tech culture. Psychology deals with a range of human concerns that are also addressed by diviners and sorcerers: fear, uncertainty, guilt, frustration, helplessness. To reject Christian psychology is to tempt people to turn to more occult sources for help. Or it is to push them in the direction of non-Christian psychology, which, like the magical worldview, will often encourage them to think that they can control their own destiny. How much better it is to provide struggling Christians with the kind of perspective described by psychologist Archibald Hart: "we desperately need the *insights* of psychology to help us *diagnose* our problems, coupled with the insights and *power* of Christianity to *solve* them."[5] Herein, if properly cultivated, lies an important "phronetic" resource.

5. Archibald D. Hart, *Me, Myself, & I: How Far Should We Go in Our Search for Self-Fulfillment?* (Ann Arbor, Mich.: Servant Publications, 1992), 9.

A Post-Therapeutic Theology

A few years ago we had a next-door neighbor, a single father, who always fought with his teenage son. Hearing their angry exchanges through the open windows was a very painful experience. A simple disagreement over misplaced car keys would quickly escalate into a major confrontation. "I hate you," he would shout at his son. "I am sorry you were ever born." The young man would reply: "I hate you too. I wish you would die!"

Sometimes I would weep when I heard these exchanges. I wished desperately that they could sit down with a therapist. Their conversations were destructive, and they were seldom really "about" the subject they were ostensibly discussing.

It struck me that I could grasp the underlying dynamics of their conversations in ways that my forebears would not have been able to. Not because I am a smarter person, or because I am equipped with more of the basics of human wisdom. Rather, I have learned much from the therapeutic culture — and much from popular therapeutic culture as I have absorbed it from TV programs, radio shows, newspaper advice columns, magazine articles, mass-market paperbacks.

Ellen Charry is right to call us to return to "classical theological psychology." But we cannot simply go back to the past. We need a post-therapeutic reappropriation of the classical tradition. We do know more about the human psyche today than our Christian forebears did. We think about abuse and stress and family systems and gender and addictions in ways that they never imagined. We cannot let go of this knowledge. But we need to fit it into a larger biblical worldview.

I once read an essay that argued that contemporary therapy is itself a "secularization" of the older Christian pietism, which paid much attention to inner states and intimate relationships. That makes sense to me. And what we now need is a "re-pietization" of secular therapy, a grounding of psychological motifs in a spiritually sensitive understanding of God's will for human beings in their wholeness. But that "re-pietization" cannot be a simple return to the past. It must absorb and incorporate and transform all that we are learning from our therapeutic culture.

The Search for Memories

Like many other people who study scholarly works about American culture, I think that one of the most important books of the 1980s was *Habits of the Heart,* by sociologist Robert Bellah and his associates. For me, an especially helpful part of that book is what Bellah and his associates have to say about *memory.* They worry that North Americans are losing their communal memories. And this loss is a very dangerous thing. Human beings, the Bellah team argues, need to participate in "communities of memory." We need stories of the past, narratives about men and women who have preceded us. We need both pleasant memories and painful ones — a healthy community will be sustained by stories not only of past successes but also of past failures. The Bellah team puts the point in strong terms: genuine communities "are *constituted* by their past."[1]

1. Robert N. Bellah et al., *Habits of the Heart: Individualism and Commitment in American Life* (Los Angeles: University of California Press, 1985), 153 (emphasis mine).

Since each of us is communal by nature, memory is also crucial to our individual well-being. We need memories of our collective past in order to sustain a healthy sense of identity as human selves. Without stories that reach back beyond our own individual pasts, we begin to shrink and shrivel up as human beings.

This is why the Bellah team, and many other students of contemporary culture, worry about what is happening to us. We are becoming spiritual amnesiacs, people without the kinds of memories that nurture and enrich our lives. Because of high divorce rates and geographic mobility, many people grow up these days without any sense of being a part of an extended family. Other bearers of communal memories — churches, ethnic-immigrant associations, neighborhood configurations, and the like — do not have the same role in our lives that they once did.

A point Paul Hiebert makes about the middle range of human concerns takes on a special significance in this regard. We need, he says, *a theology of ancestors*. This, I think, is a profound prescription. The attention paid to ancestors in folk religion — as in ancestor worship — is a way of providing a community of memory. An awareness of our ancestors gives us a sense of being a part of a larger story. It is a way of constituting our individual and collective selfhood.

We can see this need at work in the larger culture. With the loss of older ways of sustaining memories, people are looking for substitutes. New Age "channeling" is an appropriation of occult rituals for communicating with the dead. The nationalistic and ethnic rivalries that have come to the fore in the wake of communism's demise in Eastern Europe are — for all of the unspeakable cruelties that have been unleashed — often expressions of a deep desire to preserve ancestral roots.

How can we as Christians more effectively meet the need for communities of memory? I often think about this when we sing "The Church's One Foundation" in worship. What does it mean to say that we have "mystic sweet communion with those whose rest is won"? I know how Roman Catholics can answer this question — they pray directly to the saints in heaven. For many of us Protestants, however, that borders too closely on the magical.

But it is not enough for Protestants to criticize prayers to the saints, special saints' days, icons, and statues. We need to find our own ways of promoting "mystic sweet communion."

We need communal narratives about our collective past. And this need is intimately related to the importance of narrating our more personal pasts.

In an important sense, we find out who we are by being encouraged to *tell* our stories. The construction of our personal, familial, and communal narratives is itself an act of self-discovery. This is what philosophers mean, I think, when they say that "the self is *constituted* by its narratives."

The old evangelical "testimony meetings" grew out of healthy impulses. The practice of telling each other our stories ought to be sustained and even deepened in the Christian community.

But this is also a good place to emphasize again the

positive contributions of the Therapist. Good psychology can provide us with important opportunities for exploring our ancestral histories, so that we can better understand our inherited "family systems." The therapeutic setting can also serve as one of the contexts where we become better aware of "the cloud of witnesses" that surrounds us (Hebrews 12:1).

Reflection:
Help from St. Francis

In an ecumenical forum, I once debated a Catholic theologian on the subject of praying to the saints. It was a good discussion, friendly all around, although neither of us changed any minds.

Afterward a parish priest talked with me. He told me in a good-natured way that he thought I had too many scruples. "The saints help me out a lot in my ministry," he said, chuckling. Then he told me about a man in his parish who had come to him recently for help.

The man had a terrible time getting along with his mother-in-law. Thanksgiving Day was coming, and he had to spend the holiday at her home. "We always fight," he told the priest. "What can I do to get along with her for a few hours?" The priest advised him to walk into her home and give her a great big hug. "And as you get ready to do so," the priest told him, "pray this prayer to St. Francis: 'St. Francis, you hugged the leper even though

79

you found him dirty and ugly. You were able to do it because you knew that Jesus loved the leper. Help me to hug my miserable mother-in-law and show her a little bit of the love of Jesus.'"

After Thanksgiving the man came to the priest and told him that things had gone well. He had hugged his mother-in-law while praying to St. Francis. He imagined her as an ugly leper whom Jesus loved. It worked.

"You Protestants need saints too," the priest said to me. "You have plenty of people who need to learn how to hug their mothers-in-law!"

I have a few departed saints with whom I stay in touch. I never try to talk to them directly. But I do try to stay connected with their stories. One of them is Corrie Ten Boom. Every other year or so I reread *The Hiding Place*. Corrie Ten Boom's courage in identifying with Jewish people against the Nazi wickedness inspires me. I try to think of ways in which I can show a similar courage in my own life. She is a kind of nurturing Dutch grandmother to me. I live in a very different context than she did, but I want to imitate her simple and faithful love of Jesus.

But why not just imitate Jesus directly? Why do we need the "mediation" of a St. Francis or a Corrie Ten Boom? Those are good Protestant questions that get at an important concern. We do need to have a direct and personal relationship to Jesus. We must always be aware of the danger that devotion to someone else, even a very holy person who loves Jesus very much, can get in the way of our own attempts to be faithful to our Lord.

True enough. But we also need "mystic sweet communion" with others who love Jesus. That, too, is a basic requirement of the Christian life. And one very important ministry the saints can perform for us is to expand our imaginations and enrich our supply of examples of how Jesus can be loved and served. The Catholic parishioner was well served by the example of St. Francis and the leper. I am well served by being reminded of a Dutch woman's resistance to unspeakable evil because of her deep commitment to the gospel.

I am not ready to advocate rethinking our Protestant nervousness about praying *to* the saints. But I am convinced that we Protestants have to find better ways of drawing strength from the examples of St. Francis and other holy people in our collective past by keeping their stories alive. It will take conscious work — in planning our worship services and educational programs, in writing our books and articles, in the jokes we tell. And in the advice we give to people who are dreading gatherings on Thanksgiving Day.

Probing Depths

Ethnography, James Peacock tells us, "reveals the general through the particular, the abstract through the concrete." But the way we are taught by the data of human experience, he adds, is not "the way fruit flies teach about genetics," by experimentally confirming or disconfirming general hypotheses, "but in the manner of the play, the poem, or parable."[1]

Both anthropologists and psychologists do ethnography in this sense. They look for plots and subplots in the phenomena of cultural interaction and in the details of our psychic lives.

Theology must learn from these ethnographic disciplines, and especially — as I have been arguing here — in the study of popular culture. Theologians require ethnographic skills if they are to gain the instruction they need from the struggles of ordinary Christian people.

1. James L. Peacock, *The Anthropological Lens: Harsh Light, Soft Focus* (New York: Cambridge University Press, 1986), 83.

This does not mean that theologians should simply *be* anthropologists and psychologists. Theologians have their own worthy subject matter to attend to. They need to devote much of their expertise to the plots and subplots of the dramas and poetry and parables of high theology. But they also need to be informed by the ethnography of popular culture, not only to be more effective at *giving out* guidance to the larger Christian community, but also in order to *gather in* insights that are crucial to their own work.

To think about gathering in is also to remind ourselves that our ethnographic-theological efforts must always aim at *discovering truth*. In our postmodern setting, ethnography is more likely to be portrayed as a logic of invention than of discovery. For deconstructionists and their fellow travelers, meanings are not taken in; they are imposed upon the texts that we read. But Christian ethnography looks to particulars to see what they can teach us about deep and abiding realities. As Albert Borgmann notes, the postmodern fascination with particularity often focuses only on surfaces. Borgmann urges us to look even more closely at particulars than the postmodernists are inclined to do, in order to discover "the eloquence of things," to find in "the depth of the world" those "things that command our respect and grace our life."[2]

Too often we fail to investigate the deeper regions of popular religion. This is true of Christian scholars who

2. Albert Borgmann, *Crossing the Postmodern Divide* (Chicago: University of Chicago Press, 1992), 51, 82.

sometimes have little patience for popular religion. It is also often true of those many Christian leaders who are sometimes so eager to harness the energies and impulses of popular religion for the cause of Christianity that they, like their academic critics, linger too much on the surfaces; and in doing so they run the risk of merely exploiting the superficial.

We all — scholars and leaders of the "little people" — need to explore together the depths of our popular religious experience. We must probe the hidden places: looking for the signs of eloquence and grace to be found there; listening for deep calling unto deep; searching, not only for the Deeper Magic, but also for the Deeper Quests, the Deeper Pleasures, the Deeper Hurts, the Deeper Plots. And in all of this probing we need to be especially watchful, following Cardinal Newman's advice, for that practical wisdom that dwells "deep in the bosom of the mystical body of Christ."